Healthy
Eating

Milk
Butter and
Cheese

Susan Martineau
and Hel James

W
FRANKLIN WATTS
LONDON•SYDNEY

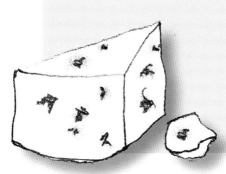

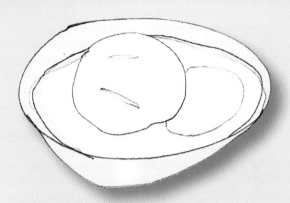

An Appleseed Editions book

First published in 2006 by
Franklin Watts
338 Euston Road
London NW1 3BH

Franklin Watts Australia
Hachette Children's Books
Level 17/207 Kent Street
Sydney NSW 2000

Created by Appleseed Editions Ltd,
Well House, Friars Hill, Guestling, East Sussex TN35 4ET

Designed and illustrated by Helen James
Edited by Jinny Johnson

ISBN-10: 0-7496-6721-4
ISBN-13: 978-0-7496-6721-4
Dewey Classification: 641.3' 7

A CIP catalogue for this book is available from the British Library

Photographs: 10 Bernard Annebicque/Corbis Sygma; 11 Chuck Savage/Corbis; 12-13 Jon Hicks/Corbis;
15 Mark E Gibson/Corbis; 16 Owen Franken/Corbis; 18 PhotoCuisine/Corbis; 21 Owen Franken/Corbis;
23 Geray Sweeney/Corbis; 24 Abbie Enock; Travel Ink/Corbis; 25 Jacqui Hurst/Corbis; 27 Robert Estall/
Corbis; 29 Adam Woofitt/Corbis.
Front cover: Adrianna Williams/Zefa/Corbis

Printed and bound in Thailand

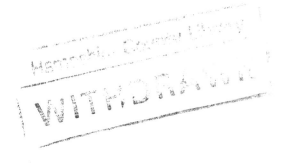

Contents

Food for health

Our bodies are like amazing machines.
Just like machines, we need the right
sort of fuel to give us energy and
to keep us working properly.

If we don't eat the kind of food we need to keep us healthy we may become ill or feel tired and grumpy. Our bodies don't really like it if we eat too much of one sort of food, like cakes or chips.

We need a balanced diet. That means eating different sorts of good food in the right amounts.

You'll be surprised at how much there is to know about where our food comes from and why some kinds of food are better for us than others. Finding out about food is great fun and very tasty!

I feel like a milkshake.

My favourite is strawberry.

Milk, yogurt and cheese help us to build strong bones and teeth.

A balanced plateful!

The good things or nutrients our bodies need come from different kinds of food. Let's have a look at what your plate should have on it. It all looks delicious!

Rice, bread and pasta

These foods contain carbohydrates and they give us energy. They are also called starchy foods. About a third of our food should come from this group.

Fruit and vegetables

Rice, bread and pasta

Bread, cheese and salad give you carbohydrates, protein, vitamins and minerals.

6

Fruit and vegetables

These are full of great vitamins and minerals and fibre. They do all kinds of useful jobs in your body to help keep you healthy. About a third of our food should come from this group.

Milk, yogurt and cheese

These dairy foods give us protein and also calcium to make strong bones and teeth.

Meat, fish and eggs

Protein from these helps your body grow and repair itself. They are body-building foods and you need to eat some of them every day.

Sugar and fats

We only need small amounts of these. Too much can be bad for our teeth and make us fat.

Milk, yogurt and cheese

Sugar and fats

Meat, fish and eggs

Water

We need to drink at least 6 glasses of water every day.

Dairy goodness

Dairy foods are made from milk. They include yogurt, cheese, butter and cream. Dairy foods give us body-building protein and calcium. Calcium is very good for us and helps us to grow strong bones and teeth.

We need some calcium every day. Milk, yogurt and cheese are the best way to get calcium. Cream and butter have a lot of fat in them so they belong in the sugar and fats part of the balanced plateful. Our bodies only need a little bit of fat.

Bone-building menu

Breakfast

Pour some milk on your breakfast cereal.

Calcium helps to keep your teeth healthy.

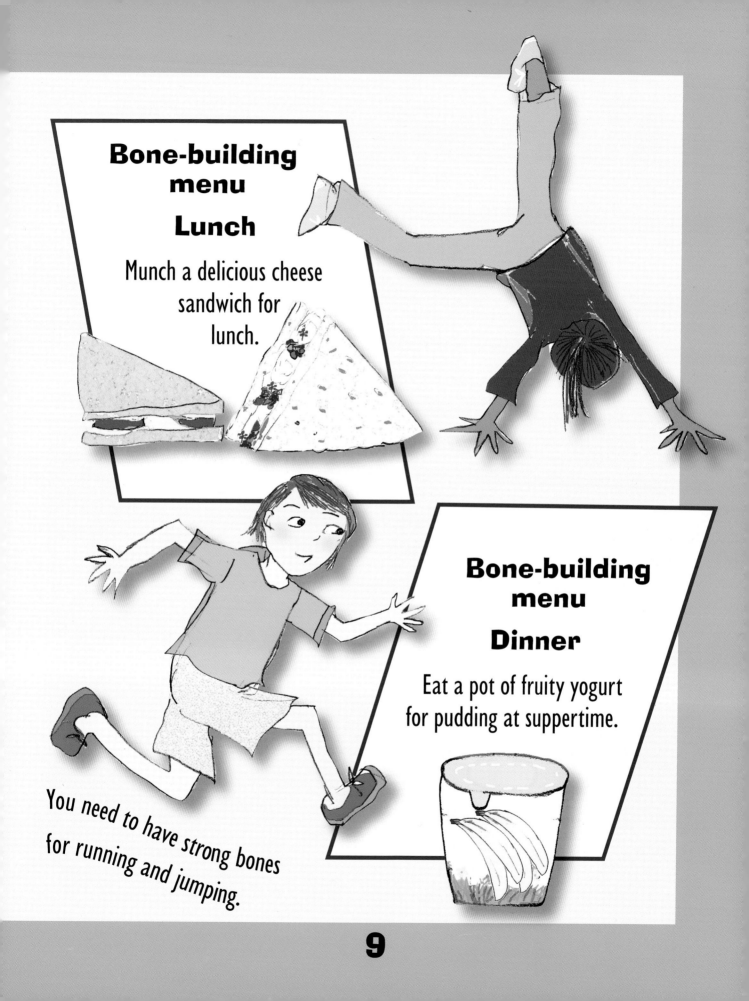

Bone-building menu
Lunch

Munch a delicious cheese sandwich for lunch.

Bone-building menu
Dinner

Eat a pot of fruity yogurt for pudding at suppertime.

You need to have strong bones for running and jumping.

Marvellous milk

Animals make milk in their own bodies to feed their babies. We can drink the milk that animals make too. Most of the milk people drink comes from cows. You can also drink milk from goats, sheep, buffalo and even reindeer!

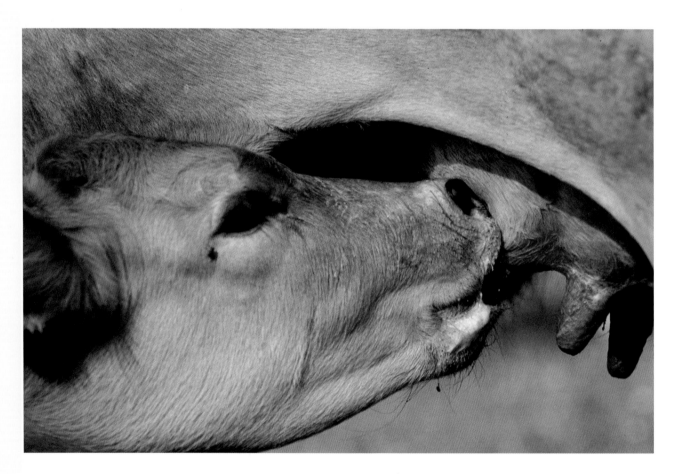

This calf will grow big and strong on its mother's milk.

From the cow to us

Farmers keep cows on dairy farms. Tubes from big machines suck the milk from the cows. The milk has to be kept very cold in a special big container. A big tanker takes the milk to a dairy.

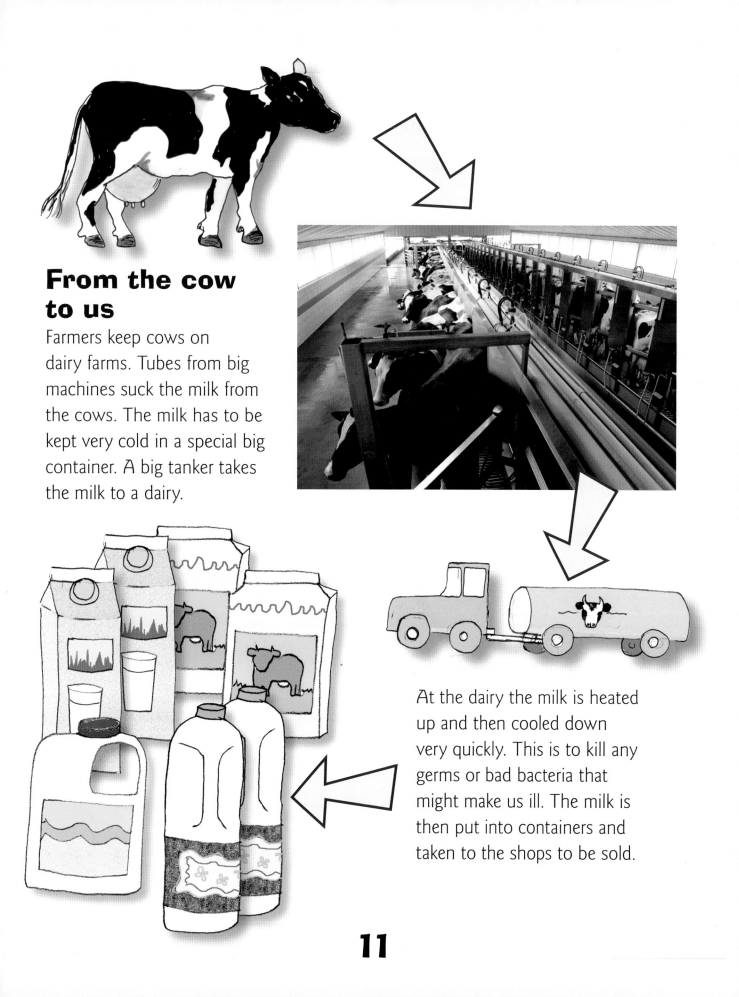

At the dairy the milk is heated up and then cooled down very quickly. This is to kill any germs or bad bacteria that might make us ill. The milk is then put into containers and taken to the shops to be sold.

Kinds of milk

Milk has fat in it and the fat is what we call cream. Before the milk is put into containers at the dairy it is processed or made into different sorts of milk with more or less fat in it.

Pancakes are a delicious way of using milk!

What about organic milk?

Some people think that organic milk is better for us.
Cows producing organic milk eat grass that has not been
sprayed with chemicals to kill bugs and weeds.

Make the most of milk

Milk is a lovely healthy drink
full of nutrients or goodness
for your body. You can use
milk in lots of other great
ways too.

Full-cream milk has
all the fat left in it.

Semi-skimmed milk has about
half the fat taken out of it.

Skimmed milk has all the fat
taken out of it.

Full-cream and semi-skimmed milk are
the best for young,
growing bodies.

Special milks

Some people cannot drink cow's milk or eat the dairy foods made from it. They are allergic to it and it makes them feel unwell. Other people just don't like the taste of milk!

Luckily you can still get protein and calcium from other kinds of milk, like the milk from goats and sheep. There is also milk made from soya beans and rice. Calcium and vitamins are added to it to make it a healthy choice. Soya milk can also be made into yogurt and cheese.

Next time you are in a food shop, have a look at the different types of milk you can buy. It's nice to know that, even if you are allergic to cow's milk, there are lots of other bone-building choices!

Whiz up a milkshake using your favourite soft fruit, like strawberries or banana, with any kind of milk you like. Just put everything in a blender or food processor and mix it well. Slurp it up!

- a big cup of milk
- a handful of fruit
- 2 tablespoons of ice cream

All kinds of cream

The fat in milk floats up to the top. You can sometimes see this in containers of full-cream or semi-skimmed milk. This fat is called cream.

When cows have been milked the cream can be skimmed off the top of the containers of milk. Like the milk, it must be heated up or pasteurized to kill any bad bacteria. After this it also needs to be kept very cold to make sure it stays fresh.

Dollops of cream on your pudding taste good but they are full of fat. That's why cream belongs in the sugar and fats part of the balanced plateful, even though it is a dairy food. Cream is delicious but it's best not to eat too much of it.

You can whisk cream into stiff peaks.

17

Pots of yogurt

Yogurt is made out of milk. It can be made from cow's milk or the milk from sheep, goats and other animals. Yogurt can also be made from soya milk. Some harmless bacteria are added to the milk. Then it is heated up and left for a few hours before being cooled down. It is put into pots ready for the shops.

Yogurt is as high or low in fat as the type of milk used to make it. It can be used instead of cream in all kinds of sweet and savoury dishes.

Check for sugar

There are lots of different kinds of yogurt in the shops – plain, fruity, low-fat, thick and creamy, Greek-style, bio-pots. But some kinds have lots of sugar in them so check the labels before you buy them.

Yogurt is lovely spooned on to a pile of fresh fruit.

Yogurt with cucumber and mint is cooling and delicious with spicy food.

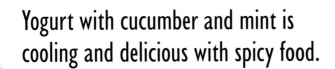

Butter and margarine

Butter is made out of cream. The cream is heated to kill any bad or harmful bacteria. Then it is put into large, revolving containers that beat and turn it. This makes all the blobs of fat in it stick together and turn into butter! Like cream, butter has a lot of fat in it and we should only eat small amounts.

Mum says not to spread the butter too thickly!

Butter is churned until it is solid. Then it can be cut into pieces, ready to be packaged and sold.

Spreads for bread

Margarine is made out of different sorts of vegetable oils. The oils are processed or 'changed' into something we can spread on our bread by mixing them with special chemicals. This often makes a kind of fat which is not very good for us.

All about oils

Oils are used to cook food or to make salad dressings and mayonnaise. Have a look at all the different kinds of oils on the shelves in the supermarket. Some are made from seeds, like sunflower oil or corn oil. Can you find any oils made from nuts?

Olive oil

Walnut oil

Sunflower oil

Corn oil

Of all the oils, olive oil is best for us. It is made out of olives and tastes delicious in salad dressings.

Olives grow on trees. They are picked by hand or with special rakes. The oil is then pressed out of them.

Know your fats!

Oils are called unsaturated fats and they are not as bad for us as fats like butter and cream. Butter and cream are called saturated fats. We do need a little bit of fat to help our bodies to use vitamins, but it is better to choose unsaturated fats.

Cheese please!

Cheese is another dairy food. It can be made out of cow's milk or the milk from other animals like goats or sheep. First the milk is mixed with special bacteria. Then another ingredient called rennet is added and this makes the milk into solid lumps called curds.

The curds are cut, shaped and pressed to make all kinds of cheeses. Some cheeses are then kept for weeks or even months before being taken to the shops to be sold. This is called ageing the cheese.

Most cheese contains quite a lot of fat but it also gives our bodies protein, calcium and vitamins.

Some cheeses do smell very strong. But they still taste delicious.

Choosing cheese

There are loads of lovely cheeses to choose from. You could do a cheese quiz with your friends to find out which one is the top favourite.

Hard cheeses

These cheeses are aged for a few weeks or months before being sold in the shops. They are great in sandwiches for your lunchbox or for making tasty cheese sauces for vegetables or pasta.

Cheddar cheese was first made in England, but it is now made in lots of other countries too.

Emmenthal cheese is from Switzerland and it has holes in it!

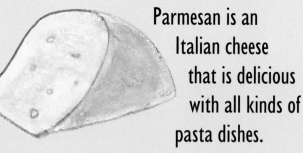

Parmesan is an Italian cheese that is delicious with all kinds of pasta dishes.

Dutch cheeses, like Edam and Gouda, have a special wax on the outside to help keep them soft and fresh.

Cheeses have to be kept at just the right temperature when they are ageing.

Blue cheeses

These cheeses are made by adding harmless bacteria or mould to them. It sounds weird but they are very tasty. Try them with bread or crackers or stir some into soup.

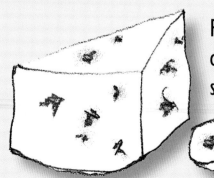

Roquefort is a French cheese made from sheep's milk.

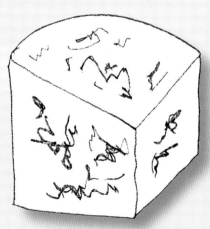

Stilton is a traditional English cheese.

Soft cheeses

Most soft cheeses do not keep for as long as hard cheeses. Soft cheeses such as Camembert and Brie do not need to be aged and should be eaten up quite quickly.

Tubs of soft cheese

There are lots of different types of white soft cheese to spread on your bread. Some of them are called 'low-fat' soft cheese and it is better to choose them.

Trick cheese!

Fromage frais is usually put on the shop shelves next to yogurts but it is really a sort of soft cheese. It was first made in France and 'fromage frais' means 'fresh cheese' in French.

Mozzarella is made from cow's or buffalo's milk and is brilliant for pizzas. It comes in the shape of a ball and needs to be kept in water.

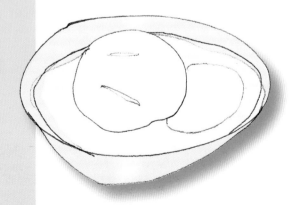

Camembert and Brie are made in France.

Words to remember

ageing   When cheese is kept for weeks or months before being sold.

allergic   This means that you feel unwell or get a rash or an upset stomach if you eat certain foods.

bacteria   Tiny creatures that are so small we cannot see them. Some bacteria are bad for us and can make us ill. Some bacteria do not hurt us and can be used to make yogurt and cheese. The bacteria in yogurt are good for our stomachs.

calcium   A mineral which helps build healthy bones and teeth.

carbohydrates   Starches and sugars in food that give us energy. Carbohydrate foods are rice, pasta, bread and potatoes.

chemicals   Substances that can be used for all sorts of things. Some, called pesticides, are used to kill weeds in fields. Some chemicals are used to process food.

curds   The solid lumps that form when milk is being made into cheese.

dairy   Place where milk is made ready for us to drink it. Yogurt, cheese, butter and cream are also made in a dairy.

fibre   Plant foods like grains and vegetables contain fibre. It helps our insides to work properly.

full-cream milk   Milk with all the cream left in it.

minerals   Nutrients in food that help our bodies work properly. Calcium is a mineral.

nutrients   Parts of food that your body needs for energy, to grow healthily and to repair itself.

organic   Grown without using chemicals to kill weeds and bugs. Organic milk comes from cows that eat grass that is not sprayed with these chemicals.

pasteurized   When milk is heated to kill any bad bacteria that could make us ill.

processed   Foods that are processed go through some changes before they reach your plate. Oils are processed to make margarine.

rennet   Rennet helps to makes the solid curd in cheese-making. Some rennet comes from the stomach of a calf. Rennet from plants is used to make vegetarian cheese.

saturated   Saturated fat is found in cream, butter and cheese as well as in fatty meat.

savoury   A savoury dish is the opposite of a sweet one.

semi-skimmed milk   Milk that has had about half the fat taken out of it.

skimmed milk   Milk that has had all the fat taken out of it.

tanker   Truck that has a large tank on it to keep milk cold while it is being taken to the dairy.

unsaturated   The sort of fat that is found in vegetable oils. It is also found in nuts, seeds and oily fish.

vitamins   Nutrients in food that help our bodies work properly.

Index

WEBSITES

General food information for all ages
www.bbc.co.uk/health/healthy_living/nutrition

Food Standards Agency – healthy eating, food labelling
www.eatwell.gov.uk

Quizzes and games on food
www.coolfoodplanet.org

Information and games on healthy eating
www.lifebytes.gov.uk/eating/eat_menu.html

Worksheets and activities
www.foodforum.org.uk

Practical advice on healthy eating
www.fitness.org.uk